Moments
for
Teens

Moments
for
Teens

by
Robert Strand

New Leaf Press

FIRST EDITION
January 1995

ISBN: 0-89221-288-8
Library of Congress: 94-73974

Cover photo by Jim Whitmer Photography, Wheaton, IL
Inside illustrations by Lin Wellford, Green Forest, AR

All Scripture references are from the New International Version, unless otherwise noted.

Every effort has been made to locate the authors or originators of the stories contained in this book. Most are the result of conversations with pastors, while others were accumulated throughout the course of a 30-year radio and television broadcasting career.

Day 1
A Famous Father

Dear Ann Landers:

A great man died today. He wasn't a world leader or a famous doctor or a war hero or a sports figure. He was no business tycoon, and you will never see his name in the financial pages. But he was one of the greatest men who ever lived. He was my father.

I guess you might say he was a person who was never interested in getting credit or receiving honors. He did corny things like pay his bills on time, go to church on Sunday, and serve as an officer in the PTA. He helped his kids with their homework and drove his wife to do the grocery shopping on Thursday nights. He got a great kick out of hauling his teenagers and their friends around to and from football games.

Tonight is my first night without him. I don't know what to do with myself, so I am writing to you, Ann. I am sorry now for the times I didn't show him the proper respect. But I am grateful for a lot of other things.

I am thankful that God let me have my father for 15 years. And I am happy that I was able to let him know how much I loved him. That wonderful man died with a smile on his face and fulfillment in his heart. He knew that he was a great success as a husband and a father, a brother, a son, and a friend. I wonder how many millionaires can say that.

15 Years Old & Lonely[1]

What a wonderful tribute written in a beautiful way. Say, when was the last time you expressed love to your father . . . or mother . . . or brother . . . or sister . . . or anybody who has impacted your life? When life is completed and over and done, the only things that are important are the relationships which we have been a part of while alive. And relationships are nurtured and grow when one of the ingredients is honest appreciation expressed. Somebody, at great personal cost, brought you into this world . . . somebody or many somebodies have contributed to your current lifestyle. When you stop and think about it, there's not much about life that we can lay claim of total responsibility to. Before you were born somebody prepared a home, yes, even a house to live in . . . roads to drive on . . . clothes to wear . . . food to eat . . . and we could go on and on!

Express appreciation before it's too late!

Today's Quote: *Everything you say and do is a reflection of the inner you.*

Today's Verse: And whatever you do, whether in word or deed, do it all in the name of the Lord Jesus, giving thanks to God the Father through Him (Col. 3:17).

Day 2
How to Become a Hall-of-Famer

When former Brave great Henry Aaron returned to Milwaukee's County Stadium on the opening day of the 1975 season to play for the Brewers, one of the first players to greet him was the team's young shortstop. "Hello, Mr. Aaron," said the 19 year old who was entering his second season as the youngest player in the majors. "I'm Robin Yount."

Mr. Yount and Mr. Aaron will undoubtedly be reunited in Cooperstown in the summer of 1998. That's when Yount, who announced his retirement at the age of 38, after 20 years with the Brewers, figures to be inducted into the Baseball Hall of Fame. But Yount, in typically laconic fashion, downplayed that prospect. "It's not my position to make that decision," he said. "I can only say I'm happy with the way my career went."

Only four men . . . Pete Rose, Aaron, Carl Yastrzemski, and Ty Cobb . . . have more big league at-bats than Yount's 11,008. He was the MVP (Most Valuable Player) at two positions, shortstop in 1982 and centerfield in 1989, and his 3,142 hits place him thirteenth on the all-time list. Once asked to name the game's three most dangerous hitters, Boston Red Sox pitcher Roger Clemens said, "Robin Yount in the first, Robin Yount in the fourth, and Robin Yount in the seventh."

At the retirement press conference, a tearful Bud Selig, the

Brewers' owner, said, "I don't think many people understand how rare it is for a player to come to a franchise, play two decades, and never cause one iota of a problem. He played the game every single day the way it's supposed to be played."

Before Christmas, Yount found himself playing golf with future Chicago White Sox minor leaguer Michael Jordan. Yount, who won the match, said, "Michael told me how great retirement was, playing golf all the time. That didn't last long. In a week or two I might go to the Bucks (Milwaukee's NBA basketball team) and ask for a tryout."[2]

To become a Hall-of-Famer isn't easy . . . and we must also acknowledge that Yount is a gifted athelete. Yet there are life lessons for all of us. Commitment to his chosen lifestyle, consistency that lasted over two decades, people relationships that worked, a team player, a role model, and a man who made a difference in his community. It's not so important how you start or what you choose to do with your life. What is important is how you finish. Life is not a sprint . . . it's a marathon!

Today's Quote: *A mind, once stretched by a new idea, never regains its original dimension again.*

Today's Verse: Trust in the Lord with all your heart and lean not on your own understanding; in all your ways acknowledge him, and he will make your paths straight (Prov. 3:5-6).

The Other Jonah

The Bible contains the story of Jonah being swallowed by a "great fish" . . . real, or just an ancient fish story? Are you sure? As recently as 100 years ago, there is record of a man who lived to tell the story after being swallowed by a whale. Here it is:

In February 1891, a young English sailor named James Bartley was a crew member of the whaling ship, *Star of the East,* which ranged in the waters off the Falkland Islands in the South Atlantic, searching for these marine leviathans.

One day, about three miles offshore, quite suddenly, the whalers spotted a sperm whale that later proved to be 80 feet long and weighed some 80 tons! Two boats with crew members and harpooners — one of them was Bartley — were sent out to get the whale. As they closed in, one harpooner catapulted his eight-foot spear toward the whale. The instant it struck, the whale twisted and lashed out with its huge tail. The tail slammed into one rowboat, lifted it into the air, and capsized it. But the sailors soon subdued and killed the wounded mammal.

When the rowboat was righted, Bartley and another crewman were missing and written off as drowned. The crew pulled the carcass of the whale alongside the ship and worked until midnight removing the blubber. The next morning, using a derrick, the sailors hoisted the whale's stomach on deck.

According to M. de Parville, science editor of *The Journal des Debats,* who investigated the incident, there was movement inside the whale's belly. When it was opened, Bartley was found on the inside, unconscious. He was carried on deck and bathed in sea water. He was confined to the captain's quarters for two weeks, because he was acting like a lunatic.

Within four weeks, Bartley fully recovered and related what it had been like to live in the belly of the whale. For the rest of his life, Bartley's face, neck and hands remained white, bleached by the whale's gastric juices!"[3]

Quite a fish story, a whale of a story, in fact. What an experience for Bartley! If he had had this experience in our day, he would be on the speaking circuit making big money, drawing huge crowds, hitting all the large churches, and writing his own book! Other than that . . . is there a moral? An application? Simply that the Bible is more than a story book. This story has been confirmed by a human experience. But how much of God's Word must be taken at face value and by faith? Without faith, the Bible says, it's impossible to please God.

Today's Quote: *The difficulty is not that we know so much, but that we know so much that isn't so.* — Ben Holden

Today's Verse: . . . the Lord provided a great fish to swallow Jonah, and Jonah was inside the fish three days and three nights (Jon. 1:17).

Day 4
Baptized by Socrates

There's an old story about a proud, arrogant young man who came to the noted philosopher Socrates asking for knowledge. He proudly walked up to the muscular philosopher and said, "O great Socrates, I come to you for knowledge."

Socrates, recognizing a pompous, thick-headed, numbskull when he saw one, asked the young man to follow him through the streets of Athens to the shores of the Mediterranean Sea. Together they waded out into the water, chest deep. Then he turned to the young man and asked, "What do you want?"

"Knowledge, O wise Socrates," said the young man with a smile.

Socrates put his strong hands on the pompous young man's shoulders and pushed him under and held him. Thirty seconds later, Socrates let him up. "What do you want?" he asked him again.

"Wisdom, O great and wise Socrates," the young man sputtered, without the smile this time.

Socrates crunched him under again . . . this time a little longer. Then he let him up, again. The young man was gasping for breath. "What do you want, young man?" Socrates asked again.

Between heavy, heaving breaths the young man wheezed, "Knowledge, O wise and wonder . . ."

Socrates jammed him under again. This time he counted to 50 before he pulled him up out of the water. "What do you want?"

"Air!" he screeched. "I need air!"

"When you want knowledge as you have just wanted air, then you will have knowledge," said a smiling Socrates.

We live in what is called the "Information Age," or a time when information and knowledge is bought and sold. Inside information can be your ticket to wealth and prestige and position. Knowledge doesn't come easily . . . it is a learning process, it takes scholarship, the application of intelligence. It's a cultivation of the mind, it's a gathering of data, it's becoming aware, it's a sharpening of perception, it's honing the memory, and comprehension as to how it can be applied. Knowledge is today's commodity! Knowledge can be your ticket to an exciting future! So . . . bottom line: How much do you really want or need knowledge? When it becomes as important as your next breath you will have it or at least the beginning of knowledge!

Today's Quote: *No one can predict to what heights you can soar. Even you will not know until you spread your wings.*

Today's Verse: If any of you lacks wisdom, he should ask God, who gives generously to all without finding fault, and it will be given to him (James 1:5).

Day 5
Greed Separates a Son from His Father

"Dear Abby" is a phenomena of our day. She seems to have an answer for all kinds of human needs and problems. The following is not from Abby, but a reader who wrote the following to Abigail Van Buren.

Dear Abby:

The letter concerning the minister who, on receiving a pair of leather gloves for services rendered, was disappointed, until he discovered a $10 bill stuffed into each finger, reminded me of this story:

A young man from a wealthy family was about to graduate from high school. It was the custom in that affluent neighborhood for the parents to give the graduate an automobile. "Bill" and his father had spent months looking at cars, and the week before graduation they found the perfect car.

Imagine his disappointment when, on the eve of his graduation, Bill's father handed him a gift-wrapped Bible! Bill was so angry, he threw the Bible down and stormed out of the house. He and his father never saw each other again. Years later, it was the news of his father's death that brought Bill home again.

As he sat one night, going through his father's possessions that he was to inherit, he came across the Bible his father had given him. He brushed away the dust and opened it to find a cashier's check, dated the day of his graduation . . . in the exact amount of the car they had chosen together.

Beckah Fink, Texas

And here is the response from Abby:

Dear Beckah: I hope Bill read the Bible cover to cover, for it contained much he needed to learn: "A foolish son is a grief to his father, and bitterness to her who bore him" (Prov. 17:25).[4]

There is not a whole lot to be added to this story . . . it says it all. Would it be fair to say that sometimes youth is wasted on the young? We get smart too late. We wake up to the lessons of life after the lesson has been experienced. Too often, it's painful. Greed is one of those passions which must be conquered early on, or it will haunt you the rest of your life. After all, how much of this world's toys can you take with you when you die? Remember that there are no U-Haul trailers behind hearses.

Today's Quote: *Selfishness is that detestable vice which no one will forgive in others and no one is without in himself.* — Henry Ward Beecher

Today's Verse: Such is the end of all who go after ill-gotten gain; it takes away the lives of those who get it (Prov. 1:19).

Day 6
An AIDS Mistake

At 18, Kaye Brown was ready for the world! The bubbly honor student was looking forward to life in the army. Last March, she signed up at a recruiting office in Houston and took a mandatory AIDS test. One week later she learned she was HIV-positive and the world was no longer a sure thing! "I was really, really angry," she says. "My career had been snatched away from me."

Though doctors estimated that she had contracted the virus recently, they recommended that she tell anyone she had had sex with in the previous year. The list was long. "It was easy for me to list the guys I had slept with," she says, "but when I counted 24, I was like, gosh!"

One former partner said, "But you don't look like you're that way."

Brown shot back, "What is that way? HIV doesn't mean that I'm dirty or low. It just means I made a mistake."

Brown blames only herself. "It makes me angry that I allowed this to happen," she says. "Choices I made have stolen away the choices that I might have had in the future."[5]

Not only will her choices be gone but her life will be taken . . . if AIDS takes its normal course of development. She has about two to four years to live, if she is fortunate and has some excellent health care.

The virus that causes AIDS is known as the human immunodeficiency virus or HIV. We do know that this virus is less infectious than others such as the virus for hepatitis B. However, once contracted there is no known cure and the result is death. From June through September, last year, there were 912 new cases among 13 to 19 year olds. There is a caution . . . these numbers are just the visible tip of the iceberg. They only include those who are in the final stages of infection with HIV. It is estimated (CDC) that between one and two million Americans are now infected with the virus. The CDC also estimates that as many as 30 percent of all AIDS-related deaths are never reported. Scary! Deadly!

We have a choice! Certain behaviors are the major cause of spreading AIDS, among them is sexual promiscuity. Let's make a choice not to indulge but to abstain . . . and the old message from God himself is to wait until marriage. Make virginity your choice! Take the moral high ground! You'll be glad you did.

Today's Quote: *Sex is worth waiting for. We must pray and speak out for a broader understanding of that fact and its importance not just to fight against the spread of HIV, but its importance to the survival of our society.* — Duane Crumb

Today's Verse: It is God's will that you should be sanctified: that you should avoid sexual immorality; that each of you should learn to control his own body in a way that is holy and honorable, not in passionate lust like the heathen, who do not know God (1 Thess. 4:3-5).

Day 7
The Freedoms of Abstinence

Bernice Krahn and Rita Salvadalena, volunteers at the Crisis Pregnancy Center, Everett, Washington, use the following "freedoms" in teaching teens to say "NO" to sexual temptations. These freedoms have been adapted from Teen Aid curriculum, by Steve Potter and Nancy Roach. Here they are:

1. FREEDOM from pregnancy and sexually transmitted disease.
2. FREEDOM from the problems of birth control.
3. FREEDOM from the pressure to marry too soon.
4. FREEDOM from abortion.
5. FREEDOM from the pain of giving your baby up for adoption.
6. FREEDOM from exploitation by others.
7. FREEDOM from the guilt, doubt, disappointment, worry, and rejection that comes with a sexual affair.
8. FREEDOM to be in control of your body.
9. FREEDOM to get to know your dating partner as a person.
10. FREEDOM to plan for the future and for the kind of life you want to live.
11. FREEDOM to respect yourself.
12. FREEDOM to be unselfish: not taking pleasure in sex at the expense of your boyfriend or girlfriend.

13. **FREEDOM** to look forward to marriage and choose and be chosen by the kind of person you will want for the mother or father of your children, without worrying about his/her learning about your sexual past.

14. **FREEDOM** to enjoy being a teenager, with many friends and boy-girl relationships.

15. **FREEDOM** from severe pain when you break up.

16. **FREEDOM** to form a strong marriage bond with one person only for life. Such couples can trust each other to be sexually faithful in marriage because both of them have practiced resisting sexual temptation before marriage.

17. **FREEDOM** to later remember your high school/college dating experiences, after you're grown up, with pleasure and happy memories, and no shame.[6]

That really says it all. You make the decision to abstain and if you ask, God will give you grace and strength! Abstinence is the answer!

Today's Quote: *What we want to say is look at the kind of love that was born on the Cross. Look at the love that cared enough to go all the way to the tomb for you. Let's give the real love a chance.* — Mark Gersmehl, Christian artist with Whiteheart

Today's Verse: Flee the evil desires of youth, and pursue righteousness, faith, love and peace, along with those who call on the Lord out of a pure heart (2 Tim. 2:22).

Day 8
Deferred Decisions

Former President Ronald Reagan learned the need of making a decision early in his teens. A kind aunt had taken him to a shoemaker to have a pair of shoes custom-made just for him. The shoemaker asked, "Do you want a round toe or a square toe?"

Young Ronald hemmed and hawed and couldn't make up his mind. So the cobbler said, "Come back in a day or two and tell me what you want."

A few days later the shoemaker saw Ronald on the street and asked what he had decided about the shoes. "I haven't made up my mind yet," the youth answered.

"Very well," said the shoemaker, "your shoes will be ready for you to pick up tomorrow."

When Reagan picked up the shoes . . . one had a round toe and the other a square toe. Says Reagan, "Looking at those shoes taught me a lesson. If you don't make your own decisions, somebody else makes them for you."

Decisions . . . decisions! Life is made up of decisions both large and small and everything in between. And while you are a teen, some of life's greatest choices must be made. Will I just finish school and get a job or do I go on to college or vocational school or trade school? Who will I live my life with? What kind of a life will I live? Will I embrace the drug culture? Will I become part of the armed services? Choices . . . decisions . . . and they just keep coming for the rest of your life.

In Guyana, 60 miles up the Essequibo River there is a village, Bartica, which serves as the supply center for the miners and prospectors working in the mountains further up the river. In the center of this village of a few thousand people there is a huge white monument placed on a concrete slab. It's impressive. It can be seen from quite a distance. Walk around the base and there is no inscription. Ask any of the citizens, and nobody knows why the monument was erected. Old-timers can't remember and the young were never told. Strange — a monument to nothing! A memorial that has no memory or meaning.

Could anything be more useless? Will your life become a momument to nothing? Right decisions will play a very important part in how useful your life will be . . . how meaningful your life can become. I want my life to count for something . . . how about you?!

Today's Quote: *The difference between a successful person and others is not a lack of strength, not a lack of knowledge, but rather in a lack of decision.*

Today's Verse: But if serving the Lord seems undesirable to you, then choose for yourselves this day whom you will serve, whether the gods of your forefathers served beyond the River, or the gods of the Amorites, in whose land you are living. But as for me and my household, we will serve the Lord (Josh. 24:15).

Day 9
You're Fired!

Have you heard the true story about a teen who went to work in a grocery store after his high-school graduation? A couple of weeks had passed and one evening his dad said, "Son, now let's talk about college."

"Oh, Dad, I didn't tell you. . . . I'm not going to go to college."

"You're not going to college? Why?"

"I'm not going to college because I have found my life's work! I'm happy!"

"What do you mean . . . you found your life's work?"

"You know," he said, "I'm driving the truck there and I love delivering groceries. The boss is happy and I just got a raise! It's really wonderful work."

"Well, son," his dad replied, "You can do something more challenging than this."

"Wait," the son returned, "didn't you tell me life is to be happy?"

"Yes."

"Well," the son said, "I'm really happy and that's what I'm going to do. I'm not going to college!" So the dad was the victim of his own myopia. He knew he'd have to use another approach.

The father went to the store and told the manager, "John, you're going to fire my son."

"What do you mean, fire your son? I've never had a young employee like him. He's the most wonderful young man I've ever hired. I just gave him a raise. He shines the truck, even . . . keeps people very happy. He's a great employee!"

"Well, he's not going on to college," said the father, "and if you don't fire him you're going to ruin his life."

The grocer had to do something. On Friday when the teen came to get his check the grocer said, "Just a minute . . . you're fired!"

"What'd I do?"

"You're fired!"

"What's wrong?"

"You're fired!"

"Wha . . .?"

"You're fired!"

This teen got the idea . . . he was fired! He came home all dejected. He met his dad and said, "All right, Dad, I'll go to college this fall." Some 30 years later, after this teen had gone on to become the president of one of the leading universities, he told his aging father, "Dad, I want to thank you for the time you got me fired!"

Today's Quote: *You become successful the moment you start moving toward a worthwhile goal.* — Unknown

Today's Verse: Listen, my son, to your father's instruction and do not forsake your mother's teaching (Prov. 1:8).

Day 10
A Leg to Stand On

Lisa Love worked hard and won a spot on the cheerleading squad during her junior year in high school. About a month later, because of cancer, she had to have her leg amputated above the knee. Over the summer, she was fitted with a prosthesis and worked hard in her physical therapy sessions and learned to maneuver and walk on it quite well. She then sought out and persuaded her cheerleader sponsor to agree to let her continue as a cheerleader. This the sponsor reluctantly agreed to, with some doubts still remaining.

Lisa worked hard on her routines by herself before school started and joined the other cheerleaders in their first practice. They were preparing for the first pep rally in the fall football season and all went well; Lisa fit right in to all the routines, without a problem.

Then came the first Thursday pep rally; the gym was packed with high school students and faculty. The cheerleading squad began their routines. Lisa started her four-step run and into a somersault across the slick gym floor. In the middle of her somersault, her artificial leg came off and skidded across the gym floor, leaving Lisa to stumble on one leg and crash to the floor. She buried her face in her hands, cried, and thought of quitting right there.

Instead, she motioned for one of her cheerleading friends to help retrieve her leg, and helped her strap that prosthesis back on. All this in front of the bleachers packed with kids. In full sight of them, she then stood straight and tall, motioned that she was ready. The squad continued their routine and Lisa performed her part of the routine to a rousing, enthusiastic, long, standing ovation![7]

Success in life has been defined as the ability to get up one more time when you have fallen down! Everybody in life has experienced failure of some kind. The question is, what do you do after you have fallen down — lay there in your tears, have your own personal pity party, feel sorry for yourself, ask, "Why has this happened to me?" or get up one more time?

About 10 percent of life is composed of the things that happen to you — 90 percent is your *reaction* to what has happened to you. If you look hard enough, you can always blame somebody else for your problems . . . maturity is taking responsibility for yourself and your reactions in life. Plus, there is another resource available: When we stumble or loose a leg, Jesus Christ stands ready to help you re-attach what has been lost. All of heaven is ready for your standing ovation.

Today's Quote: *In the end, the only people who fail are those who do not try.*

Today's Verse: Therefore, since we are surrounded by such a great cloud of witnesses, let us throw off everything that hinders and the sin that so easily entangles, and let us run with perseverance the race marked out for us (Heb. 12:1).

Day 11
Your Sins Will Find You Out

The following story has been making its rounds through the upper Pacific Northwest area. Truth or not, I can't verify.

The story begins with this pathetic teenage boy sitting huddled by a beach fire on the chilled Pacific coast of the state of Washington. Lo and behold, a game warden appeared out of the nearby woods, approached the fire, and asked the youth what he was doing.

He said, "I am roasting a sea gull for my dinner. I haven't eaten in a couple of days."

The warden said, "What? A sea gull? You can't do that. Don't you know there is a law against killing sea gulls? They are a crucial part of our eco-system here. They help keep the beaches clean. I'm going to cite you and it's a pretty stiff fine."

The young man pleaded, "Oh, come on, man, it's just one sea gull. And I'm hungry and I'm out of work. What's one lousy sea gull compared to one really hungry human? I had to leave my family and go look for work and I haven't been able to find anything. Please don't cite me. I don't have any money so they'll have to throw me in jail."

Well, the warden was touched by the story and began to weaken this one time. He said, "Okay, I'll let you go this time . . . but, be sure it doesn't happen again." At this the warden turned and started to walk off. Then, he turned back and asked, "By the way, I'm curious. What does a roasted sea gull taste like, anyhow? I've always kinda wondered."

The young man looked up from chewing on the bird's carcass to say, "Oh, it's a real different kind of taste, somewhere between the flavor of a Snowy White Owl and an American Bald Eagle."

Oh, well . . . what more need I say? As we scratch around in this story, the moral begins to take shape. It's straight out of God's Book. "Be sure your sins will find you out." That promise is about as intimidating and awesome as any from the Bible. More than that, it's frightening in its implications. Who wants to be found out? Not very many people who have done wrong. Why do people run away, go into hiding, change identities? Among other things . . . to hide from the truth being known about them. So what we are hiding *can* hurt us.

There really is only one answer to trying to cover up our sin problem. There is no way it can be covered . . . but it can be forgiven and removed and remembered against us no more! Who can do that? How can it be done? If your past is a problem, how about a few moments spent in asking God for His help to remove that sin? He hears and He forgives, and only He can remove the sin from your life.

Today's Quote: *You will never know that Jesus is all you need until Jesus is all you've got.* — Mother Teresa

Today's Verse: He that covereth his sins shall not prosper: but whoso confesseth and forsaketh them shall have mercy (Prov. 28:13;KJV).

Day 12
The Different Perspective

The story is told about a freshman who was trying out for a college football team but there was a problem . . . the coach wasn't too impressed with his intelligence. He told him quite frankly that he didn't think he was smart enough to play football. The young man pleaded to be given a chance to prove himself. So the coach finally relented and said, "I'll make you a deal. I'll give you a test. In fact, I'll let you take the test home and think about it and if you can pass it tomorrow morning, I'll let you try out for the team. There are only three questions on the test. First, figure out how many seconds there are in a year. Second, tell me the name of the two days in the week that begin with 'T,' and third, tell me how many D's there are in the song, 'Rudolph the Red-Nosed Reindeer.'"

So the young man said he'd go home and think about it. Sure enough, he was back to see the coach bright and early the next morning.

The coach said, "Okay, here we go. First question, how many seconds are there in a year?"

The young man smiled and said, "Coach, I figured that one out. There's 12." The coach looked puzzled and asked how he figured that.

The hopeful player said, "There are 12 seconds in the year, Coach . . . January 2nd, February 2nd, March 2nd, April 2nd, May 2nd . . ."

The coach said, "Okay, that's not what I had in mind, but I'll accept that. How about question number two, what are the names of the days of the week that start with 'T'?"

He came back with, "Oh, that's easy . . . today and tomorrow."

The coach was again impressed even though that wasn't what he'd had in mind. He said, "Okay, here's the last one, how many 'D's' are there in the song, 'Rudolph the Red-Nosed Reindeer'?"

The young man brightened and replied, "Oh, I know that one . . . there's 138!"

The coach was now really puzzled and asked, "How in the world did you figure that?"

The prospective, eager, potential football player immediately started counting on his fingers and began chanting the familiar Christmas tune, 'De De, De De De, Dee Dee, De De De De De De De. De. . . .'"

That's so bad I couldn't even find anybody who wanted to claim to be the source. But, really, there are other ways of doing things that can bring a fresh and delightful perspective in life. It's called *staying out of the rut of normal thinking*.

Today's Quote: *The pleasure you get from your life is equal to the attitude you put into it.*

Today's Verse: See, the former things have taken place, and new things I declare; before they spring into being I announce them to you (Isa. 42:9).

Wooden Shoes, Velvet Slippers, and Silk Pajamas

Harry Emerson Fosdick is credited with the observation that history is filled with the sound of wooden shoes climbing up the stairs and velvet slippers walking down. The famous jockey Eddie Arcaro made the same point when he confessed that he found it really tough to get up at 5 a.m. to ride and exercise horses once he started wearing silk pajamas. Humanly speaking, the prize tends to go to those who want it most and work the hardest for it.

Comfort takes over creativity. Security becomes a stronger passion than challenge. Velvet slippers and silk pajamas don't bring to mind such people as Daniel Boone, Lewis and Clark, or Thomas Edison. Some historians have claimed that the Roman Empire fell because its people took too many baths!

The sound of wooden shoes on the stairs can still be heard all over the world. Tragically, there is somewhat of a haunting feeling in the United States and perhaps in Canada, that we have peaked. It's nothing for a 19 year old, upon applying for a first job, to inquire about vacation benefits and the company's retirement plan. A senior pastor tells of a recent seminary graduate whom he was interviewing for a ministry staff position making it clear that he would only work a five-day, forty-hour week. And any evening work would have to be compensated for by time off during the day.

A variety of conclusions could be drawn from our present subject. This much is for sure: NOTHING STAYS WON! It's always easier for people and nations to struggle than it is for them to arrive. Out of the depths we cry to God . . . but from the heights, it's hard to see the need for prayer. When life makes it easy to believe in God, it's hard to believe in God. Part of it comes from our having to deal with people and our own attitudes that velvet slippers and silk pajamas are a sign that God is pleased with us and wants us to enjoy a time of ease.[8]

Life does not always yield secrets to the most gifted or the most talented or the best looking, but will to those who are persistent, committed, and willing to work and not give up too soon. Work is a therapy, struggle can be the vehicle through which lifestyle changes can come about. When life is a challenge, reaching a goal is much more appreciated. There is never a time when we have arrived. It's a marathon, not a sprint. So . . . welcome the struggle! Go after the prize! Increase your desire! Go for it!

Today's Quote: *Excellence can be attained if you constantly strive for perfection, and you care enough to do your very best in everything, in every way.*

Today's Verse: Woe to you who are complacent in Zion, and to you who feel secure on Mount Samaria . . . (Amos 6:1).

◈◈◈

The Winning Attitude

Kelley Roswell, age 11 (at this time), is a Little League softball player. She plays shortstop and pitcher for the Grand Mesa Major girls all-stars. She loves softball. She can hardly wait for springtime to roll around so she can get back on the field to play.

That's not all. Kelley is an outstanding student in school and refuses to settle for anything less than an "A" in any of her classes.

Kelley is young, and normally people this young don't deserve the label of "hero," but in my estimation she is very deserving. I don't think she can be considered an ordinary girl.

Kelley Roswell, age 11, has leukemia. Since it was diagnosed in March of 1988, she has been in a life-and-death battle with the disease. She has "ALL," otherwise known as "Acute Lymphocytic Leukemia (commonly known as childhood leukemia). As a result, she traveled to Denver, Colorado, and spent weeks in the Children's Hospital in earnest battle for her life. She had to return to Denver from Grand Junction (500 miles round trip) every week for a time. This was reduced to a return trip every six weeks. The four-hour trips, injections, transfusions, and pills . . . all have been taken in stride by Kelley, without complaint. Normally, chemotherapy has the side effects of vomiting and nausea, but according to her father, Steve, she's had no major problems; she has yet to get sick from the treatment.

Mother Joanne said, "As a mother, I could be weepy, but Kelley hasn't allowed that. God gave us Kelley and we've learned that the time we have with her is special. God's had His hand on Kelley. God gives us children as gifts and they belong to Him. We get them for only a certain amount of time." The Roswells are a committed Christian family, members of the First Assembly of God in Grand Junction. Prayers have been a great help in this battle. The church and community have been sources of strength and support.

Even leukemia didn't slow Kelley in playing her beloved softball. For example, during the summer of 1988, she just didn't slow up; she's a real star, pitching and hitting her team to a second place finish! Any way you look at it, Kelley's a winner.[9]

And . . . I can tell you, Kelley beat her cancer! She's disease-free, today! How do I know? I was her pastor during this ordeal. She's really a winner any way you look at it!

Today's Quote: *I can believe that one day every bruise and every leukemia cell and every embarrassment and every hurt will be set right, and all those grim moments of hoping against hope will be rewarded.*
— Phillip Yancey

Today's Verse: That is why, for Christ's sake, I delight in weaknesses, in insults, in hardships, in persecutions, in difficulties. For when I am weak, then I am strong (2 Cor. 12:10).

Day 15
The Bullfighters' Resolve

In Costa Rica, the traditional Spanish/Mexican bullfight has undergone some important changes that distinguish it from what a tourist would be able to see in Spain or Mexico. The Costa Ricans no longer allow the toreador to kill the bull during the classic fight.

As a result, there has been a drastic plunge in the quality of Costa Rican bullfighters.

No longer do any of the good or great bullfighters stop in to fight in Costa Rica. And further, no native bullfighters are really being developed. Therefore, the Costa Ricans have altered their fights to allow anyone who is 18 or older and sober to fight the bull.

It's quite a spectacle, even comedic. Many of the bullfights begin with as many as 100 to 150 young men dressed in bullfighting clothes, holding the cape, standing proudly in the ring, waving to the crowd, enjoying the attention. At the sound of the trumpet . . . all turn, waiting for the bull to break wildly through the gate of the chute.

When the bull enters, snorting, pawing, looking for something to charge . . . immediately, most of the would-be bullfighters scramble wildly over the sides of the ring to safety. The bull makes the first charge . . . and more scramble over the side.

From that beginning mob of so-called "toreadors," just a few are really ready to challenge the bull. All want the name of "BULL-

FIGHTER," but only a few will receive it. Many want the glory of the moment . . . but very few are willing to go through the preparation and practice that it takes to become a bullfighter. They are nothing but pretenders.

In life you will come across lots of people who can talk the talk . . . but can't walk the walk. Here's where the rubber meets the road and the boys are separated from the men and the girls are separated from the ladies. It's about maturity and coming through when the chips are down. It's being there time and time again.

Teddy Roosevelt said it better than I can: "The credit belongs to those who are actually in the arena, who strive valiantly; who know the great enthusiasms, the great devotions, and spend themselves in a worthy cause; who at the best, know the triumph of high achievement; and who, at the worst, if they fail, fail while daring greatly, so that their place shall never be with those cold and timid souls who know neither victory or defeat."

Let's be the real thing!

Today's Quote: *Some succeed because they are destined to, most succeed because they are determined to.*

Today's Verse: So do not throw away your confidence; it will be richly rewarded. You need to persevere so that when you have done the will of God, you will receive what he has promised (Heb. 10:35-36).

Day 16
I Wish I Had Known

A man of full, ripe, mature years, and well-preserved, was asked to speak before a group of young people to share his wisdom. He was to provide the reflection of years, which is an impossible experience for the younger folks. Here is the message that was given:

Having passed the first twoscore and ten years of my life, and realizing that the more sand that has escaped from the hourglass of life, the clearer we should see through it, I find myself more prone to meditate and philosophize.

My life has been rich. But there have been regrets, regrets which you, too, will experience in time. These can largely be grouped as "Things I wish I had known before I was 21."

I wish I had known that my health after 30 was largely dependent on what I had put into my stomach before I was 21.

I wish I had known how to take care of my money.

I wish I had known that a man's habits are mighty hard to change after the age of 21.

I wish I had known the world would give me just about what I deserved.

I wish I had known the folly of not taking the advice of older and much wiser people.

I wish I had known you cannot get something for nothing.

I wish I had known what it meant to Mother and Father to raise a son.

I wish I had known more of the helpful and inspiring parts of the Bible.

I wish I had known that there is no better exercise for the heart than reaching down and helping people up.

I wish I had known that the "sweat of my brow" would earn my bread.

I wish I had known that a thorough education brings the best of everything.

I wish I had known that honesty is the only policy, in dealing with my neighbors, and also in dealing with myself and with God.

And today I wish I knew the formula for impressing you and other young people that life is a mirror which will reflect back to you what you think into it.

Today's Quote: *Why can't life's big problems come when we are teenagers and know everything?* — Unknown

Today's Verse: I returned, and saw under the sun, that the race is not to the swift, nor the battle to the strong, neither yet bread to the wise, nor yet riches to men of understanding, nor yet favour to men of skill; but time and chance happeneth to them all (Eccles. 9:11;KJV).

Day 17
Rising Above Fear

Following the success of her book, *The Joy Luck Club*,[10] the first-time novelist Amy Tan feared that she might be type-cast. "I didn't want to be the mother/daughter expert," she says. "So I tried something else until I realized that rebellion was not a good reason to write."

Then, suddenly, her mother provided inspiration for her next project. "I knew she had lived a harsh, repressed life in China. I asked about World War II and she said, 'I wasn't affected.' Then she mentioned that when the bombs fell, 'We were always scared they would hit us.' I pointed out that she had said she wasn't affected. 'I wasn't,' she replied. 'I wasn't killed.' " That statement became a revelation. Tan's goal became to understand this difference between her perspective on life and her mother's life-perspective.

Later, during the Tiananmen Square uprising, Amy wrote the book, *The Kitchen God's Wife*,[11] based on her mother's life. Amy Tan then said, "I wanted to know what it is like to live a life of repression, to know the fear, and what you must do to rise above the fear."[12]

Did you really catch that last statement — what you must do to rise above fear! Fear is an enemy that can reduce any of us to jelly. What is the secret to overcoming fear? There is a major clue to be found in God's Word (the Bible) . . . read it through and see if you can find the 365 "fear nots." There is one for every day of the year!

Fear has all kinds of dimensions, from dread to outright terror!

Fear comes in all sizes and different kinds of packages. Now, some fear is needed to survive in life . . . without some healthy fear you'd step off the curb into the path of a speeding car or put your hand on a hot stove.

Let's try some on for size. Ailurophobia, fear of cats; algophobia, fear of pain; androphobia, fear of men; bathophobia, fear of falling from high places; ergasiophobia, dislike of work; and so on. Scientists who study human beings say there are at least 30 different kinds of fear. Fear is an enemy that must be conquered.

Did you know that Joseph Stalin was one of the unhappiest men to ever live on our planet, as well as being a man plagued by fears? He was nearly paralyzed by his fears. He had eight different bedrooms built in the Kremlin in which he could be locked up like a bank vault. Nobody knew which of these eight he would select to spend the night in. Too much fear can cause lots of life's problems.

God says to you, "Do not be afraid!"

Today's Quote: *In the middle of every difficulty lies opportunity.*

Today's Verse: So do not fear, for I am with you; do not be dismayed, for I am your God. I will strengthen you and help you; I will uphold you with my righteous right hand (Isa. 41:10).

Day 18
Schwarzkopf's Leadership Principles

General H. Norman Schwarzkopf gained prominence as the commander of the U.S. forces in the Persian Gulf War. In a recent interview with *INC.* magazine, the General shared his leadership principles:

1) You must have clear goals and you must be able to articulate them clearly to others.

2) Give yourself a clear agenda. Every morning, write down the five most important things to accomplish that day, and get those five done.

3) Let people know where they stand.

4) What's broken, fix now. Don't put it off. Problems that aren't dealt with lead to other problems.

5) No repainting the flagpole. Make sure all the work your people are doing is essential to the organization.

6) Set high standards. People won't generally perform above your expectations, so it's important to expect a lot.

7) Lay the concept out, but let your people execute it.

8) People come to work to succeed. So don't operate on the principle that if they aren't watched and supervised, they'll bungle the job.

9) Never lie. Ever.

10) When in charge, take command. Some leaders who feel they don't have adequate information put off deciding to do anything at all.

The best policy is to decide, monitor the results, and change course if it is necessary.

11) Do what is right. The truth of the matter is that you always know the right thing to do. The hard part is doing it.[13]

When I read these "Schwarzkopf Principles" my first thought is *Where did they come from? Who was the major influence in his life? How did he come to believe what he believes? How young was he when he began to formulate life principles?*

Most of us tend to put off such thinking about life. We're waiting for all the conditions to be just right before we begin living. You know, the bottom line is that life is what happens to you while you are waiting for life to begin. Formulate your own life philosophy and then live by it. By not thinking through these issues, you are creating a lifestyle for yourself.

Today's Quote: *The quality of a person's life is in direct proportion to their commitment to excellence, regardless of their chosen field of endeavor.*

Today's Verse: Do not let this Book of the Law depart from your mouth; meditate on it day and night, so that you may be careful to do everything written in it. Then you will be prosperous and successful (Josh. 1:8).

Day 19
The Goal Is the Goal

Bobby Dodd, the former great football coach of Georgia Tech, tells the story of a game in which his team was leading 7 to 6 with just a minute to go. He instructed his quarterback NOT to pass the ball under any conditions! He said, "Whatever you do, hold on to that football; DO NOT PASS THE BALL!"

In the next few seconds of play they moved the ball down the field to within 10 yards of the opposing team's goal line. As the quarterback began to execute the next play, with seconds ticking away, he just couldn't resist and he threw a pass!

As too often happens, the pass was intercepted by a player on the other team. This opponent began the 90-yard run toward the Georgia Tech goal line. The entire Tech team had given up the chase . . . except the quarterback who had thrown the interception. He continued to chase his opponent and somehow overtook him and tackled him, causing a fumble which the quarterback managed to recover just short of their goal line! That was the last play of the game!

Georgia Tech won the game 7 to 6. After the game, the losing coach said to Coach Dodd, "I will never understand how your quarterback was able to do what he did."

Dodd explained, "Well, it's actually quite simple . . . your man was running for a touchdown; my quarterback was running for his life!"[14]

While we're on football stories, did you hear about the coach who said, "Remember, football develops individuality, initiative, personality, and leadership. Now, get in there and do exactly as I tell you!"

Can you take one more? This coach was dejected and desperate because his team was losing 42-0. He looked down the bench at his subs and finally picked on Henderson. "Henderson, if I sent you in, do you think you could get ferocious?"

"Sure thing, coach," he said. "Just one thing. What number is this guy Ferocious?"

Oh well . . . is it possible that some of life's lessons can also be learned on the football field or in an athletic endeavor? I think so. Let's go for it!

Today's Quote: *If one advances confidently in the direction of their dreams, and endeavors to lead a life which they have imagined, they will meet with a success unexpected in common hours.* — Henry David Thoreau

Today's Verse: Make it your ambition to lead a quiet life, to mind your own business and to work with your hands, just as we told you, so that your daily life may win the respect of outsiders and so that you will not be dependent on anybody (1 Thess. 4:11-12).

Day 20
The Switch

A young trial lawyer had developed a reputation for himself within a short time of being an accomplished and shrewd attorney. His courtroom techniques had been polished to the finest detail. His opponents feared him; his clients loved him. He was sure to win each case. He began writing in law journals, and invitations to speak about his techniques began to appear. After a number of these he developed a standard lecture to be used for these audiences.

He traveled with his chauffeur, a bright young man who was proud to be associated with this renowned lawyer. After months of listening to the same lecture, the brash young chauffeur announced that he had heard the same speech so many times that he could give it himself. This so intrigued the lawyer that the switch was arranged.

It was agreed that the next time they were out of town and no one would recognize them, they would exchange duties. The lawyer dressed as the chauffeur and drove the limo to the banquet hall while the chauffeur, dressed like the lawyer, was introduced to a room full of expectant lawyers.

The chauffeur waxed eloquent, demonstrating techniques and addressing details with precision. At the end of the speech the chauffeur was given a standing ovation. It was a magnificent talk. The moderator indicated there were still a few minutes left and asked the appreciative audience if they had any questions for their honored guest.

One lawyer ventured to ask a question concerning the legal precedents for one of the techniques referred to earlier in the speech. The lawyer, dressed as the chauffeur, in the back of the room felt his heart sink. He could easily field the question, but there was no way to let his chauffeur know the answer. They were about to be exposed!

The chauffeur asked the questioner to repeat the question. After listening to the question a second time, the chauffeur chuckled. With just a slight tinge of mockery he responded, "Why, that's such a simple and well-known precedent that all of you should know that! The common layperson should also know the answer. In fact, to demonstrate my premise, I am going to let my chauffeur give you the answer."

How's that for quick thinking on your feet? And another lesson in life-preparation. Some things look easy on the surface and can be duplicated or copied. But when the real questions come, that's where that schooling and experience pays off. That's the real thing . . . let's not take any short-cuts because sooner or later you will be found out.

Today's Quote: *A certain amount of opposition is a great help to any person. Kites rise against, not with the wind.*

Today's Verse: But in your hearts set apart Christ as Lord. Always be prepared to give an answer to everyone who asks you to give the reason for the hope that you have. But do this with gentleness and respect (1 Pet. 3:15).

Day 21
To Catch a Hog

Many years ago, in the Smokey Mountains of Tennessee, some domesticated hogs escaped from a farmer's pen. Over a period of several generations of hogs, these pigs became wilder and wilder until they were a menace to anyone who crossed their path. A number of skilled hunters tried to locate and kill them, but the hogs proved to be too elusive.

One day an older man leading a small donkey pulling a cart came into the village closest to the habitat of these wild hogs. The cart was loaded with lumber and grain. The local citizens were curious about what he was going to do. He told them he had come "to catch them wild hogs." They laughed in disbelief that the old man could accomplish what the local hunters were unable to do.

Two months later the old man returned to the village and told the citizens that the hogs were trapped in a pen near the top of the mountain. The village people coaxed him into telling them how he had accomplished such a feat.

"First thing I done was find the spot where the hogs came to eat. Then I put a little grain right in the middle of the clearing. Them hogs was scared at first but curiosity finally got to them and the old boar started sniffing around. After he took the first bite the others joined in and I knew right then and there I had them."

"Next day I put some more grain out and laid one plank a few feet away. That plank kind of spooked them for awhile, but that free lunch was a powerful appeal. It wasn't long before they were back eating. All I had to do was add a couple of boards each day until I had everything I needed for my trap. Then I dug a hole and put up my first corner post. Every time I did something they'd stay away a spell. But they always came back to eat."

"Finally, the pen was built and the trapdoor was set. Next time they came to eat they walked right into the pen and I sprung the trap."[15]

The point is obvious . . . when you make any creature dependent upon something, it no longer has the need or will to make its own way. The same thing happens to young people. Sin's enticing pleasure pulls at us long enough to create the habit and we are caught! A government handout can do the same . . . taking away all incentive to work for our living. But with any handout also comes bondage and dependence and laziness and ultimately, entrapment . . . and then it's too late!

Today's Quote: *Better shun the bait than struggle in the snare.* — John Dryden

Today's Verse: The thief comes only to steal and kill and destroy; I have come that they (you) may have life, and have it to the full (John 10:10).

Day 22
Persistence

He was only 18 and badly in need of a job when this young man read an ad in a Boston newspaper: "Wanted, young man to learn stock-brokerage business. P.O. Box 1720, Boston, Massachusetts."

He carefully prepared a letter and answered the ad, emphasizing his interest in the job. But he received no reply. He wrote again . . . no reply. He wrote a third time, but still no reply.

His next plan of action was a trip to the main post office in Boston where the postal box was located. He asked for the name of the holder of Box 1720, but the clerk on duty refused to give out this information. The young man then asked to see the postmaster. No go — no name of the boxholder because it was against policy to divulge this information.

What to do now? Then the thought came to the young man as to how he could find the information he desired. He set his alarm for 4:00 a.m., got his own breakfast, and took the early morning train to Boston. He arrived at the post office about 6:15 a.m. and staked out a watch near Box 1720. It was a long wait, but finally a man appeared who went over to the box with key in hand and took out the contents. The young man followed at a discreet pace to the destination. It was a stock-brokerage firm. The young man entered and requested to see the manager of the firm.

The young man told the manager how he had made application for the advertised job three times, with no response. Then of his trip to the post office to attempt to find out the name of the boxholder.

Before he could finish his story the manager interrupted him by asking "But how did you find out that it was our firm with the advertisement?"

The persistent young man replied, "I stood in the lobby of the post office near Box 1720 for several hours. Then when your man came in to get the mail from the box, I simply followed him to your office."

The manager smiled as he said, "Young man, you are exactly the kind of persistent person that we are looking for. Innovative, too. Welcome to our firm, you are now an employee!"

Persistence is a quality that wins the prize. Anything of value in this life that is worth going after demands the quality of persistence. Persistence is nothing more or less than seeing your goal and then keeping on with the pursuit until that goal is reached. Be persistent!

Today's Quote: *There aren't any hard-and-fast rules for getting ahead in the world . . . just hard ones!* — Paul Lee Tan

Today's Verse: But none of these things move me; nor do I count my life dear to myself, so that I may finish my race with joy, and the ministry which I received from the Lord Jesus, to testify to the gospel of the grace of God (Acts 20:24;NKJV).

Day 23
More Than Whoop-de-do

Dr. James Dobson (Focus on the Family) tells this story as it was told to him by his mother about the high school she attended.

Her high school was in a small Oklahoma town and it had fielded a series of very sorry, pathetic football teams. Losing was the norm for them, especially if it was a big game. Consequently, it affected not only the student body but the whole community . . . they were tired and depressed from this Friday night debacle of losing.

Finally a wealthy oil man could take it no longer. After another disastrous game, he asked the coach if he could make a locker room talk to the team. It had to be one of the most stirring speeches of all time. Certainly this team had never heard anything like that. This was the deal: to every boy on the team, to every coach . . . if they won, they would each be given a brand new Ford! All they had to do was win the next game — the game against their arch rivals. This was more than inspiring words . . . it was a hard offer! Think of it . . . a brand new Ford!

As you might expect, the team went nuts, slapping each other on the back, cheering, and otherwise carrying on. For seven days the team ate, drank, and breathed football. And when they slept, they dreamed of touchdowns and rumble seats. Of course the offer became public knowledge and the high school contracted a holiday-like fever. Each member of the team imagined himself in the driver's seat of a sharp little coupe with "girls in the front and girls in the back."

Finally it was time for the big game. The team assembled in the locker room; the atmosphere was electric. The remarks from the coach seemed anti-climactic. The team hurried out to face the enemy. They circled up at the sidelines, put out their hands, and shouted "Rah, rah, rah!" Then they went out onto the field . . . to be demolished, 38 to 0!

All the energy, the exuberance, the whoop-de-do, didn't amount to a single point on the scoreboard! A week of jumping and dreaming could not make up for a lack of discipline, coaching, talent, and character. Emotion, by itself, is not enough to prepare you for the battles of life. Feelings will let all of us down and leave us looking more than a bit foolish if that's all we depend on to accomplish life's tasks. Emotion, however, added to discipline, practice, knowledge, wisdom, character-building, a willingness to pay the price, and to delay gratification, can be the icing on the cake of life! Enthusiasm is great . . . but it takes more than just emotion to win big in life!

Today's Quote: *It is true that if we abandon ourselves unreservedly to our emotional impulses, we often render ourselves incapable of doing any work.* — Andre Maurios

Today's Verse: For all seek their own, not the things which are Jesus Christ's (Phil. 2:21).

Dear Ann Landers:

I was a compulsive liar who started young. Although my parents did all they could to stop it, I kept lying. My problem was trying to impress people. My life never seemed glamorous enough. Here is a short history of what happens to a liar:

I went through school lying to my friends, trying to be a big shot. When I graduated I had no friends, so I started to look for new ones. By then lying was a way of life.

In order to support the lies I needed more money than I had, so I wrote checks I couldn't cover. I also impersonated a naval officer and later a successful businessman. My wife found out that I had totally misrepresented myself and invented friends and businesses I never had. She left me. The same thing happened with my second wife. I decided I had to change. Shortly after I married my third wife, I went to prison for passing bad checks. She divorced me while I was in prison.

This advice is for the kid who lies. Please think about the future. A lie not only hurts you, but it poisons all your relationships.

I'll get out of prison some day, and when I do I vow to tell the truth. I will probably still be called a liar, but after a while people will find out that they can trust me. I'm now 26, and by the time I'm 50, I will have built a good reputation. A kind teacher once told me that a person's word is worth more than gold. It's too bad that it took me so long to wake up.

If you are a liar, stop while you still have friends. I hope my letter will help somebody who is where I was about 15 years ago.

Steve M. in Oregon, Wisconsin

Pretty sobering when we can see a whole lifestyle condensed down to a tragic letter like this one. If you are not a liar . . . don't become a liar. If you are a liar . . . stop. How many lies does it take to become a liar? If you have told a lie or lived a lie . . . is it possible to have that erased from your record? Yes! Ever hear of the word, "forgiveness"? Only God can forgive sin and lying because, ultimately, all sin is against God. How to be forgiven? Ask Him! Forgiveness is His to give . . . His grace and mercy removes the sin . . . but it's our responsibility to humble ourselves, admit the problem, and ask for forgiveness.

Today's Quote: *This above all: to thine own self be true, and it must follow, as the night the day, Thou canst not then be false to any man.* — Shakespeare, *Hamlet*

Today's Verse: You shall not give false testimony against your neighbor (Exod. 20:16).

Day 25
How High Can It Fly?

Do you remember your first helium-filled balloon? Did it happen at the fair, or carnival, or on the streets of your city, or was it at a parade? You clutched it with joy, maybe it was tied to your wrist. It was fun! It wanted to always go up. What fun with a balloon! Then . . . somehow, it slipped out of your hand, maybe you cried, as it went up . . . up . . . up, until it finally went out of sight, taken by the wind. Could it have been your first physics lesson learned the hard way? Now . . . did you ever wonder how high up that balloon really could have gone?

There is an answer provided for us from the "National Scientific Balloon Facility" located in Palestine, Texas. That little latex balloon would have eventually reached a height of approximately 18,000 feet! As it climbed, expansion would have taken place. At the 18,000-foot level, the helium inside would have expanded to about 80 percent more than its original volume. This is about the absolute limit of the latex to expand, and that little balloon would have burst!

What if you wanted to sail a balloon beyond that height? How can it be done? There are specially designed experimental balloons that can reach heights of more than 120,000 feet! These specially built balloons have been designed with ducts which vent off the expanding pressure of the gases as the balloon rises. Pretty clever.

So what's the difference in a plain ordinary latex balloon and an experimental balloon that can soar to unbelievable heights? The balloons we cherished as kids have a limited ability to expand and adapt while the others are designed for expansion.

It's much the same thing in life . . . some of us might be destined to blow apart with only a little pressure. But there are others who have prepared themselves for new heights, and because of the adaption and design will be able to withstand the pressures of life on the climb.

Life holds out fantastic possibilities for those who are willing to make preparation. Nobody plans to fail . . . especially when you look at life through the eyes of youth. Based on life insurance industry statistics you can take 100 people who are now in their late teens and look ahead to age 65 making these predictions:

1 will end up independently wealthy

4 will have all the money they need and be comfortable

5 will still be working to earn their living

36 will have died

54 will depend on family, friends, or the government for a living

Today's Quote: *If you would not be forgotten, either write things worth reading or do things worth writing about.* — Ben Franklin

Today's Verse: . . . one thing I do: Forgetting what is behind and straining toward what is ahead, I press on toward the goal to win the prize for which God has called me heavenward in Christ Jesus (Phil. 3:13-14).

Day 26
Nothing Could Beat Me

This happened in the 10,000 meter race at the Olympics in Munich, Germany. Entered in this race was a young man from Finland by the name of Lasse Viren. Nobody expected him to even place in this race. He wasn't listed among the top 15 runners in the world. He was literally a nobody when it came to this distance. But he had trained for the Olympics and committed himself to this grueling event.

Over 85,000 people were present in the stadium. The gun went off signaling the start, and 75 men took off to run 25 laps — about 6 1/2 miles. Lasse Viren took off with the pack for this greatest race of a lifetime. It was his big chance! About 2 1/2 laps into the race, with elbows and legs flying, the man who was expected to win was hit and thrown off the track. When he was hit he was knocked unconscious. In his fall he also knocked Viren to the track, head over heels. How would you like that? Ten years in training and then an accident like that in the biggest race of your life.

Viren, however, jumped back up to his feet and with confidence began running to catch up with the pack. The crowd sensed the drama unfolding before them and was soon on its feet shouting encouragement. They could not believe what they were seeing. Viren kept on running. He caught the last man, and kept running until he caught up with and passed the leaders in the pack to cross the finish line first to set a new Olympic record in the 10,000 meter race!

Later, Lasse Viren was interviewed by the press and he told them he found out that if he could be knocked down and win, nothing could beat him!

I believe the reason he won was because of the shock of being knocked down. It's like a shock treatment! Under the stress of the race and the double tragedy of the fall, he used reserve energy that would have been released in no other way. What does falling or failure do to you or in you? Do you go down to stay or do you bounce back for another try?

I love the courage of attitude as shown to us by a little old lady. She was frail, too. And she had lost the sight of one of her eyes which had to be removed. When it was to be replaced with a false eye, she said to her doctor, "Young man, when you select that new eye for me, be sure and choose one with a twinkle in it!" I love it, don't you?

Today's Quote: *Following the path of least resistance is what makes people and rivers crooked. People seldom drift to success!* — Dick Underdahl-Pierce

Today's Verse: Be strong and take heart, all you who hope in the Lord (Ps. 31:24).

Day 27
Attack!

Supposedly this is a true story . . . but the source has been lost or misplaced. Could it have been one of those "Paul Harvey" stories? It is reported to have been written up in a small town newspaper.

There was a burglar who was casing the homes in one particular neighborhood, trying to find his next target. He especially was looking for houses that would be left unguarded by people leaving for vacation. He slowly cruised until he saw a family loading their suitcases and goodies into their family van. He parked a block away and watched until everything had been loaded and the van packed with kids and luggage pulled out of the drive.

He left and returned after dark and approached the front door and rang the bell. Of course there was no answer, but he was just checking. Then the burglar neatly picked the lock and let himself in. He called into the darkness, "Is anybody home?"

He was absolutely stunned when he heard a voice reply, "I see you and Jesus sees you."

Terrified, the burglar called back, "Who's there?"

Again the voice came back, "I see you and Jesus sees you."

Deciding to not run so quickly, the burglar switched on his flashlight and aimed it in the direction of the voice. To his great relief, his light revealed a caged parrot reciting the refrain, again, "I see you and

Jesus sees you." The burglar laughed out loud. "I see you and Jesus sees you."

The burglar heaved a sigh of relief, his heart slowed down, he caught his breath. Then the burglar reached over and switched on the light. THEN he saw it! Beneath the parrot's cage was a huge Doberman Pinscher, mouth open, softly growling.

Then the parrot said, "Attack, Jesus, attack!"

The story was revealed by the burglar himself from the emergency room of the local hospital where extensive stitches were used to close up the many wounds.

We chuckle and think of the poetic justice meted out, "Serves him right!" Funny, yes . . . but there is a truth here, too. At all times we are being observed by others, yes; but even more closely by God. Even the darkness can't hide us from His omniscience. Sobering, thought-provoking, and it makes you think. Not only are we being observed, but we will be asked, someday, to give an account of how we have lived this life.

Today's Quote: *The mouth is the grocer's friend, the dentist's fortune, the orator's pride, and the fool's trap. — Sunshine Magazine, 8/73*

Today's Verse: Where can I go from your Spirit? Where can I flee from your presence? If I go up to the heavens, you are there; if I make my bed in the depths, you are there (Ps. 139:7-8).

Day 28
Earthquakes and Questions

Terror struck that April morning in 1906 when the San Andreas Fault settled, shaking San Francisco to the ground! While thousands of panic-stricken refugees struggled to get out of the burning city, a man with rumpled hair, keen eyes, and a hawk-like nose rode into the city on the only train to reach it that day.

He was William James, the famous psychologist who was then in his sixty-fourth year and suffering from a severe heart condition. For the next 12 hours James scrambled amid roaring flames, falling buildings, and piled rubble. He had a notebook in hand, all the while eagerly asking the fleeing inhabitants, "How did you feel when the shaking began?" He then proceeded to ask, "What thoughts flashed through your mind?" and concluded with, "Did your heart beat faster?"

This was the passion and drive that made Will James one of the foremost scientists of his generation. His thirst for truth caused him to explore, experiment, change, and grow. He had an insatiable curiosity to learn about every facet of the human personality and all he could about the secrets of life and living.

Tragically, the difference between scientists like William James and some religionists is, the scientist openly admits he does not possess all of truth and passionately seeks it. On the other hand, too many religionists sit smugly claiming they have the answer to all of life's problems. Because of this attitude, some thinking people have looked upon religion as arrogant ignorance and there is very little about it which seems appealing. It really doesn't take much of a genius to know there are many unanswerable problems to life, and even Paul, the great Apostle, freely admitted, "We see through a glass darkly."

Life and Christianity have great areas of questions that have not been answered at this point. What an adventure awaits us as we continue to explore the new areas yet unexplored. The Bible tells us that we are to "seek to excel." This is in the use of the gifts of the Holy Spirit, but the application can also be made for other areas.

Explore the Word of God, devour it for life's answers. Become a sharp student and develop your powers of observation. Ask questions. Look for answers. There are new truths for you to discover from the Bible.

Today's Quote: *The greatest discovery of this twentieth century is the fact that whatever the mind of man can conceive and believe, man can achieve!* — William James

Today's Verse: Do your best to present yourself to God as one approved, a workman who does not need to be ashamed and who correctly handles the word of truth (2 Tim. 2:15).

Day 29
Who You Are Makes a Difference!

A teacher in New York decided to honor each of her seniors in high school by telling them the difference they each made. Using a process developed by Helice Bridges of Del Mar, California, she called each student to the front of the class, one at a time. First she told them how the student made a difference to her and the class. Then she presented each of them with a blue ribbon imprinted with gold letters which read: "WHO I AM MAKES A DIFFERENCE."

Afterward, the teacher decided to do a class project to see what kind of impact recognition would have on a community. She gave each of the students three more ribbons and instructed them to go out and spread this acknowledgment ceremony. Then they were to follow up on the results and report back to the class in about a week.

One of the boys went to a junior executive in a nearby company and honored him for helping him with his career planning. He gave him the blue ribbon, two extra ribbons, and said, "We're doing a class project on recognition, and we'd like you to go out, find somebody to honor, and give them a blue ribbon, then give them the extra ribbon so they can acknowledge a third person to keep this acknowledgment ceremony going. Then please report back to me and tell me what happened."

Later that day the junior executive went to his boss, a grouchy fellow. He sat his boss down and told him he deeply admired him for being a creative genius, and then asked him to acknowledge someone else with the remaining ribbon.

The boss was greatly surprised to receive the honor. That night he came home and said to his 14-year-old son, "The most incredible thing happened to me today. One of the junior executives came in and told me he admired me and gave me a blue ribbon for being a creative genius. Imagine! I started thinking about whom I would honor and I thought about you. I want to honor you. My days are hectic and when I come home I don't pay a lot of attention to you. Sometimes I scream at you for not getting good grades or leaving your room in a mess . . . but somehow, tonight, I just wanted to let you know that you do make a difference. Besides your mother, you are the most important person in my life. You're a great kid and I love you!"

The startled boy started to sob and sob and couldn't stop crying. His whole body shook. He looked up through his tears and said, "I was planning on committing suicide tomorrow, Dad, because I didn't think you loved me. Now I don't need to."[16]

Today's Quote: *We need four hugs a day for survival. We need eight hugs a day for maintenance. We need 12 hugs a day for growth.* — Virginia Satir

Today's Verse: Do not withhold good from those who deserve it, when it is in your power to act (Prov. 3:27).

Day 30
Who Is on Your Wall?

It was a night at home, quiet, a time for some reading in front of the fireplace. I picked up the current issue of *Sports Illustrated* and as is my custom turned to the tidbit section, I believe it used to be called the "Scorecard" section. It's where short, interesting little stories of sports people from all around the globe are reported.

My attention was focused on the tragic story of Rico Leroy Marshall, an 18-year-old senior at Forestville High School in Glenarden, Maryland. Rico was a basketball star with everything going his way . . . a promised athletic scholarship to the University of South Carolina, first place winner in his school's talent contest, and he was one of the most popular kids in school.

That's background, here's the story . . . Rico was driving home from a high school basketball game on a Friday night when he was stopped by a county sheriff in a patrol car. On the seat of the car beside Rico was a plastic bag with several chunks of crack, the highly-concentrated and addictive form of cocaine. So that he wouldn't be arrested for illegal possession, he swallowed the drugs as the sheriff made his way to the stopped car. Later that night he went into convulsions. His parents rushed him to the hospital, but early on Saturday morning Rico Leroy Marshall died of a drug overdose.

One more element appears in this story . . . on the wall of Rico's bedroom, was a huge poster of his hero . . . basketball star, Len Bias. Bias was the star of the University of Maryland basketball team and for that year was the #1 draft pick for the NBA (National Basketball Association). He was chosen by the Boston Celtics. But on the night he was drafted #1 . . . Len Bias died of an overdose of cocaine!

A very sad story? Yes! Are you surprised? Maybe not. But consider . . . Rico's role model was Len Bias. I can only imagine that one of the first things he saw in the morning and the last thing at night before closing his eyes was Len. Len was the hero, role model, dream, goal of Rico.

Now my question to you: Who is your role model? Who is on the poster in your bedroom? Who would you like to follow? When you are dreaming of your future, who is the one person that comes to your mind, who do you see? Who do you have pasted on the inside of your locker door? Who is on the dash of your car? Who do you want to be like? Choose well! Heroes are important . . . but even more important is the hero you choose to follow.

Today's Quote: *I've always wanted to be somebody, but I should have been more specific.* — Lily Tomlin

Today's Verse: Let us fix our eyes on Jesus, the author and perfecter of our faith . . ." (Heb. 12:2).

Notes

1. Ann Landers, "Dad's Wisdom Grows with Age . . . Yours," *Chicago Tribune,* 6/17/90.
2. Steve Wulf, *Sports Illustrated,* 2/21/94, condensed.
3. Anonymous, Parables, Etc., 10/93, Platteville, CO.
4. Dear Abby, *The News-Leader,* Springfield, MO, 9/93.
5. *Newsweek,* 8/3/92.
6. Alice Kalso, "World," from *Parables, Etc.,* 9/88.
7. Larry Pillow, *Parables, Etc.,* 12/90, adapted.
8. Ernest Campbell, *Campbell's Notebook,* 10/88, adapted.
9. Jeff Letofsky, *Daily Sentinel,* Grand Junction, CO, 7/17/88.
10. Amy Tan, *The Joy Luck Club* (New York, NY: Ivy Books, 1989).
11. Amy Tan, *The Kitchen God's Wife* (New York, NY: G.P. Putmans Sons, 1991).
12. Mervyn Rothstein, *New York Times,* adapted.
13. Norman Schwarzkopf, *Ministry Advantage,* Nov./Dec., 1992, Fuller Institute.
14. George Maronge Jr., *Parables, Etc.,* 2/93.
15. Zig Ziglar, from a motivational talk.
16. Helice Bridges, chairperson of the Board for Difference Makers, Inc., Del Mar, CA, condensed.

Moments to Give series

Moments for Mothers

Moments for Fathers

Moments for Graduates

Moments for Christmas

Moments for Each Other

Moments for Teens

Moments for Grandparents

Moments for Pastors

Moments for Teachers

Moments with Angels

$9.95 each

Available at bookstores nationwide,
or for more information call 1-800-643-9535